THINKING
ON YOUR B

© 2009 by Barbour Publishing, Inc.

ISBN 978-1-60260-377-6

Text without credits is taken from *Little Birthday Surprises, May Your Birthday Be Filled with the Promise of Good Things to Come, Happy Birthday, A Birthday Celebration, On Your Birthday, 365 Simple Pleasures, Pass-Along Promises: Inspiration for Women, Pass-Along Promises: Inspiration for All Occasions, 365 Everyday Prayers,* and *365 Stress-Free Moments for Women.* Published by Barbour Publishing, Inc.

Published by Barbour Publishing, Inc., P.O. Box 719, Uhrichsville, Ohio 44683 www.barbourbooks.com

Our mission is to publish and distribute inspirational products offering exceptional value and biblical encouragement to the masses.

 Member of the
Evangelical Christian
Publishers Association

Printed in China.

THINKING OF YOU
ON YOUR BIRTHDAY

BARBOUR
PUBLISHING

I'm thinking of you on your birthday. . .
and I'm wishing for you the best
of everything the future holds.

It's faith in something and enthusiasm for something that makes a life worth living.

OLIVER WENDELL HOLMES

Delight yourself in the Lord
and he will give you the
desires of your heart.

PSALM 37:4 NIV

I'm wishing you
the unexpected on
your special day.

Don't ever save anything for a special occasion. Being alive is the special occasion.

UNKNOWN

Life is short.
Be swift to love;
make haste to be kind.

HENRI F. AMIEL

Take care of the minutes
and the hours, and the years
will take care of themselves.

UNKNOWN

Do not let trifles disturb your tranquility of mind. . . . Life is too precious to be sacrificed for the nonessential and transient. . . . Ignore the inconsequential.

GRENVILLE KLEISER

God will never, never, never let
us down if we have faith and
put our trust in Him.
He will always look after us.

MOTHER TERESA

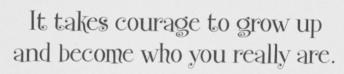

It takes courage to grow up
and become who you really are.

E. E. CUMMINGS

Lord, I want to reach my true potential and become the person You created me to be. Show me how I can best put my unique gifts, circumstances, and relationship with You to use in ways that will make a positive difference in this world. Amen.

The future is as bright
as the promises of God.

WILLIAM CAREY

If we celebrate the years behind
us they become stepping-stones of
strength and joy for the years ahead.

UNKNOWN

The LORD will guide you always; he will satisfy your needs. . . . You will be like a well-watered garden, like a spring whose waters never fail.

ISAIAH 58:11 NIV

I am always content with
what happens, for I know that
what God chooses is better
than what I choose.

EPICTETUS

Count your age by friends,
not years. Count your life
by smiles, not tears.

I thank You, Father God,
for the many years
You have given me.

The greatest use of life
is to spend it for something
that will outlast it.

WILLIAM JAMES

The mere sense of
living is joy enough.

EMILY DICKINSON

On your special day. . .
may you discover a flower
in a sidewalk crack.

Cherish all your happy moments;
they make a fine cushion for old age.

BOOTH TARKINGTON

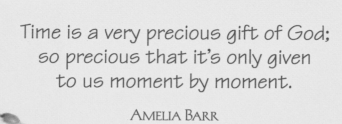

Time is a very precious gift of God;
so precious that it's only given
to us moment by moment.

AMELIA BARR

Let us not hurry so in our pace of living that we lose sight of the art of living.

FRANCIS BACON

Life is what we make it.
Always has been, always will be.

GRANDMA MOSES

I pray that you will know
the full goodness of life.

If wrinkles must be written upon
our brows, let them not be written
upon the heart. The spirit
should never grow old.

James A. Garfield

Joyfulness keeps the heart
and face young.

ORISON SWETT MARDEN

Take pleasure in your age!
God has new things to show you
at every age; He has delights and
insights, wonders and fulfillment,
planned for each year of your life.
So take pleasure in the age
you are right now.
It's the perfect age for you to be.

Every person's life is a fairytale
written by God's fingers.

HANS CHRISTIAN ANDERSON

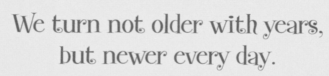

We turn not older with years,
but newer every day.

EMILY DICKINSON

And in the end, it's not the
years in your life that count.
It's the life in your years.

ABRAHAM LINCOLN

Our lives are filled with simple
joys and blessings without end;
And one of the greatest joys
in life is to have a friend.

The Lord has richly blessed you!

Dear friend, I pray that you may enjoy good health and that all may go well with you, even as your soul is getting along well.

3 JOHN 1:2 NIV

It is lovely when I forget all birthdays, including my own, to find that somebody remembers me.

ELLEN GLASGOW

Celebrate each new
day in your life. . . .
Imagine the possibilities!

The story of living goes on
perpetually. The days and the
years inevitably turn the pages
and open new chapters.

LILIAN WHITING

I joy to see myself now live:
This age best pleaseth me!

ROBERT HERRICK

Everything God creates
tells how glorious He is—
everything, even you.

PAMELA McQUADE

That I am here is a
wonderful mystery to which
I will respond with joy.

Where the soul is full of peace
and joy, outward surroundings
and circumstances are of
comparatively little account.

HANNAH WHITALL SMITH

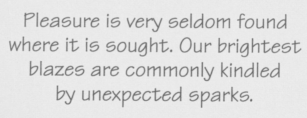

Pleasure is very seldom found
where it is sought. Our brightest
blazes are commonly kindled
by unexpected sparks.

SAMUEL JOHNSON

Today, I'm praying that you will. . .have a wonderful day!

Your birthday is a good day to look back at the years that have passed and reflect on all that God has done in your life. Notice the patterns He created over the years. Celebrate the memories of love that fill your life. Rejoice in the years' achievements.

I wish you all the joy
that you can wish.

<small>WILLIAM SHAKESPEARE</small>

Today's bright moments are
tomorrow's fond memories.

Father, You have given me all I
need to live a joyful life, and I rejoice
in Your gifts of beauty. Amen.

You are a part of the great plan,
an indispensable part. You are needed;
you have your own unique share
in the freedom of Creation.

MADELEINE L'ENGLE

Happiness is found along the way,
not at the end of the road.

Take time to laugh—
it is the music of the soul.

As we grow in our capacities to
discover the joys that God has placed
in our lives, life becomes a glorious
experience of discovering
His endless wonders.

Surely goodness and love will
follow me all the days of my life,
and I will dwell in the house
of the Lord forever.

Psalm 23:6 NIV

I wish for you the knowledge
that you are loved.

Know that you are special and loved by the One who created the stars in the night sky.

The heart that loves
is always young.

GREEK PROVERB

May your footsteps set you upon a
lifetime journey of love. May you wake
each day with God's blessings and
sleep each night in His keeping.
And may you always walk
in His tender care.

I pray that you will spread
God's light with all the unique
gifts He created in you.

No eye has seen, nor ear heard,
nor the human heart conceived,
what God has prepared for
those who love him.

1 CORINTHIANS 2:9 NRSV

I'm so glad God made you!

It is God to whom and with whom
we travel; and while He is the end
of our journey, He is also at
every stopping place.

ELISABETH ELLIOT

God has a purpose for
your life, and no one else
can take your place.

I wish for you new
adventures this year.

Think of it—not one whorled finger
exactly like another! If God should take
such delight in designing fingertips,
think how much pleasure the unfurling
of your life must give Him.

LUCIE CHRISTOPHER

God grant you many happy years,
Till, when the last has crowned you,
The dawn of endless days appears,
And heaven is shining around you.

OLIVER WENDELL HOLMES

May your memories be
birthday gifts of joy.

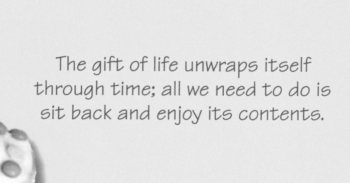

The gift of life unwraps itself
through time; all we need to do is
sit back and enjoy its contents.

Never lose an opportunity of
seeing anything that is beautiful;
for beauty is God's handwriting—
a wayside sacrament. Welcome it in
every fair face, in every fair sky,
in every fair flower, and thank God
for it as a cup of blessing.

RALPH WALDO EMERSON

Help me, Lord, to recognize
each blessing You've given
with a gratitude-filled heart.

The best things are nearest:
breath in your nostrils, light in
your eyes, flowers at your feet,
duties at your hand, the path
of God just before you.

ROBERT LOUIS STEVENSON

You can never measure what
God will do through you.

OSWALD CHAMBERS

God is the one who enables us
to find joy in this moment—
just as it is, just as we are.

May there always be work for your hands to do. May your purse always hold a coin or two. May the sun always shine on your windowpane. May a rainbow be certain to follow each rain. May the hand of a friend always be near you, and may God fill your heart with gladness to cheer you.

IRISH BLESSING

I want you woven into a tapestry
of love, in touch with everything
there is to know of God.

Colossians 2:2 MSG

When we're conscious of the
treasure of Himself that God
placed in us, we're fully alive.

The patterns of our days are
always changing. . .rearranging. . .
and each design for living is unique. . .
graced with its own special beauty.

Take time this year to slow down,
to make space in your life for peace.
And even in the busiest,
most frantic days this year holds for
you, my prayer is this: May the Holy
Spirit's peace dwell undisturbed
within your heart.

[God]. . .surrounds me with love
and tender mercies. He fills
my life with good things.

PSALM 103:4–5 NLT

If I had a single flower for
every time I think about you,
I could walk forever in my garden.

CLAUDIA GRANDI

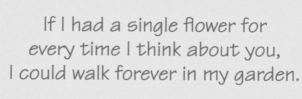

I'm praying that you will. . .
take delight in the
future's promise!

I'm praying that you will. . .
enjoy your memories of the past!

The private and personal blessings
we enjoy. . .deserve the
thanksgiving of a whole life.

JEREMY TAYLOR

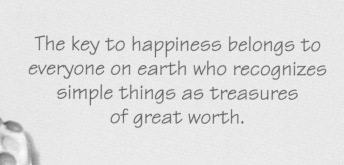

The key to happiness belongs to
everyone on earth who recognizes
simple things as treasures
of great worth.

We are born to have a
connection with God.

CLEMENT OF ALEXANDRIA

Don't let yourself get so busy that you miss those little but important extras in life—the beauty of a day. . . the smile of a friend. . .the serenity of a quiet moment alone. For it is often life's smallest pleasures and gentlest joys that make the biggest and most lasting difference.

I wish for you joy
in each passing year.

I asked God for all things that I might enjoy life. He gave me life that I might enjoy all things.

UNKNOWN

The wonder of living is held within the
beauty of silence, the glory of sunlight,
the sweetness of fresh spring air,
the quiet strength of earth,
and the love that lies at the
very root of all things.

UNKNOWN

Rejoice! Be glad! Celebrate!
Joy is one of God's gifts.

ELLYN SANNA

You have made known to me the paths of life; you will fill me with joy in your presence.

ACTS 2:28 NIV

Add to your joy by
counting your blessings.

Keep your face upturned to
Him as the flowers do the sun.
Look, and your soul shall love and grow.

HANNAH WHITALL SMITH

Every person's life is a fairy tale
written by God's fingers.

HANS CHRISTIAN ANDERSON

I wish for you a sense of achievement
as you become the person
God made you to be.

There will never be anyone like you.
Allowing *God* to fulfill His
purpose in you is the miracle for
which you were created.

Thou art my hope, O Lord GOD:
thou art my trust from my youth.

PSALM 71:5 KJV

Embrace the wonder and excitement
each day brings. For tomorrow
affords us new opportunities. . .
time to experience. . .time to create. . .
time to reflect. . .time to dream.

K. WILLIAMS

Every moment is full of wonder,
and God is always present.

It is astonishing how
short a time it takes for very
wonderful things to happen.

FRANCES HODGSON BURNETT

Live fully each
moment of every day!

Live your life while you have it.
Life is a splendid gift—there
is nothing small about it.

FLORENCE NIGHTINGALE

God is good to one and all;
everything he does is
suffused with grace.

PSALM 145:9 MSG

Lord, fill my heart with light as
Your blessings fall upon me and
I grow closer to You. Amen.

"I have loved you with an everlasting love; I have drawn you with loving-kindness."

Into all our lives, in many simple, familiar, homely ways, God infuses this element of joy from the surprises of life, which unexpectedly brighten our days, and fill our eyes with light.

HENRY WADSWORTH LONGFELLOW

May God send His love like
sunshine in His warm and gentle way,
To fill each corner of your heart
each moment of today.

Treat yourself with
loving-kindness.

God created a marvelous,
incredibly detailed work in you.

PAMELA MCQUADE

I will praise You, for I am fearfully and wonderfully made; Marvelous are Your works, And that my soul knows very well.

PSALM 139:14 NKJV

Happiness consists more in small
conveniences or pleasures that occur
every day, than in great pieces
of good fortune that happen
but seldom to a man in
the course of his life.

BENJAMIN FRANKLIN

If you can eat today, enjoy the
sunlight today, mix good
cheer with friends today,
enjoy it and bless God for it.

HENRY WARD BEECHER

On your special day. . .
may you do something that
makes you feel like a kid again.

We were not sent into this world to do anything into which we cannot put our hearts.

JOHN RUSKIN

Everyone has a unique role to fill
in the world and is important in
some respect. Everyone, including
and perhaps especially you,
is indispensable.

NATHANIEL HAWTHORNE

The consciousness of loving and being loved brings a warmth and richness to life that nothing else can bring.

OSCAR WILDE

When we do the best we can,
we never know what miracle
is wrought in our life or
in the life of another.

HELEN KELLER

Aliveness in God is addictive.

NANCY GROOM

Within each of us, just waiting
to blossom, is the wonderful
promise of all we can be.

Being confident of this, that he
who began a good work in you will
carry it on to completion until
the day of Christ Jesus.

PHILIPPIANS 1:6 NIV

Before me, even as behind,
God is, and all is well.

JOHN GREENLEAF WHITTIER

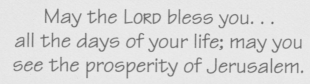

May the LORD bless you. . .
all the days of your life; may you
see the prosperity of Jerusalem.

PSALM 128:5 NIV

Happiness is as a butterfly, which, when pursued, is always beyond our grasp, but which, if you will sit down quietly, may alight upon you.

NATHANIEL HAWTHORNE

When you look back on the years
God has ordained for you, what will
you see? I pray that you will be able
to find joy and beauty in the most
trivial of things, because you
have spent those precious
minutes with God.

LORI SHANKLE

Each new thought of
you makes me smile.

Let all thy joys be as
the month of May,
And all thy days be as
a marriage day:
Let sorrow, sickness,
and a troubled mind
Be stranger to thee.

FRANCIS QUARLES

Time is a wonderful gift given
to us by God—so don't fear the
passing years. Celebrate them!

This is the true joy in life,
the being used for a purpose
recognized by yourself
as a mighty one.

GEORGE BERNARD SHAW

Every experience God gives us,
every person He puts into our lives,
is the perfect preparation for the
future that only He can see.

CORRIE TEN BOOM

Write it on your heart
that every day is the best
day of the year.

RALPH WALDO EMERSON

Blessed are those who give
without remembering and receive
without forgetting.

<small>Unknown</small>

Celebrate yourself! You are a unique creation of God. In all the world, there's no one else like you. . . . Praise God for all the gifts He gave the world when He created you.

Every good and perfect
gift is from above.

JAMES 1:17 NIV

Think. . .of the world
you carry within you.

RAINER MARIA RILKE

The best things in life, the truly
precious things, get better with time;
each year only increases their value.
Your life is like that, too!

The here and now is
no mere filling of time,
but a filling of time with God.

JOHN FOSTER

Make use of time,
let not advantage slip;
Beauty within itself
should not be wasted.

WILLIAM SHAKESPEARE

Birth may be a matter of a
moment, but it is a unique one.

FREDERICK LEBOYER

God, who got you started in
this spiritual adventure. . .will never
give up on you. Never forget that.

1 CORINTHIANS 1:9 MSG

Every day is a brand-new opportunity
to offer our hands, our hearts,
our time, and our resources. . . .
It is the giving of ourselves
that makes life rich.

BONNIE JENSEN

On your special day. . .
may you receive an answer to prayer.

Ask, and ye shall receive,
that your joy may be full.

JOHN 16:24 KJV

A prayer, in its simplest definition,
is merely a wish turned heavenward.

PHILLIPS BROOKS

God made today just for you!

I try to avoid looking forward
or backward, and try to
keep looking upward.

CHARLOTTE BRONTË

God has designed you wonderfully well. He thinks about you every minute of every day.

LORI SHANKLE

Whatever is lovely. . .
think about such things.

PHILIPPIANS 4:8 NIV

Life is a mirror; if you frown at it,
it frowns back; if you smile,
it returns the greeting.

WILLIAM MAKEPEACE THACKERAY

Be a life long or short,
its completeness depends on
what it was lived for.

UNKNOWN

Contentment is a perfect
condition of life in which no aid
or support is needed.

JOSEPH HENRY THAYER

Nothing contributes more to cheerfulness than the habit of looking at the good side of things.

WILLIAM B. ULLATHORNE

Life is God's novel.
Let Him write it.

Isaac Singer

You are precious to God,
and today He celebrates your life.
Why not join the celebration? Rest in
the assurance that God is doing great
things in your life. Know that you are
loved and treasured by the
Creator of the universe.

God has a special purpose just for you—that only you can fill. Remember, on this special day, you are loved!

LORI SHANKLE

A little of what you
fancy does you good.

MARIE LLOYD

Celebrate your years!
Be grateful for all the gifts
time has given you.

There is something satisfying, rejuvenating, comforting about the seasons. They remind me that I play one small part in a much bigger picture—that there is a pulse, a sequence, a journey set into motion by the very hand of God Himself.

KAREN SCALF LINAMEN

God has meaning and purpose for each season of your life—and with each birthday milestone, you can celebrate all He's taught you.

I wish for you special blessings
for the chapters of your life,
which have yet to be written.

"The earth is the Lord's,
and everything in it."

1 CORINTHIANS 10:26 NIV

We should all do what, in the long run, gives us joy, even if it is only picking grapes or sorting the laundry.

E. B. WHITE

Rest is not idleness, and to lie
sometimes on the grass under trees
on a summer's day, listening to the
murmur of the water, or watching the
clouds float across the sky, is by no
means a waste of time.

Sir John Lubbock

The simple fact of God's
presence with us makes our joy.

HANNAH WHITALL SMITH

It is one of the most beautiful compensations of life, that no man can sincerely try to help another without helping himself.

RALPH WALDO EMERSON

The joy that you give to others
is the joy that comes back to you.

JOHN GREENLEAF WHITTIER

Some people weave burlap into
the fabric of our lives, and some weave
gold thread. Both contribute to make
the whole picture beautiful and unique.

UNKNOWN

You are a blessing!

My heart rejoices
in knowing you!

On your special day. . .may you
experience something that reminds
you that angels are watching over you.

A person should hear a little music,
read a little poetry, and see a fine
picture every day of their life, in order
that worldly cares may not obliterate
the sense of the beautiful which God
has implanted in the human soul.

JOHANN WOLFGANG VON GOETHE

Today I am wishing you
a day filled with delight.

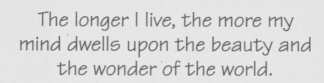

The longer I live, the more my
mind dwells upon the beauty and
the wonder of the world.

JOHN BURROUGHS

You can't do anything about the length of your life, but you can do something about its width and depth.

EVAN ESAR

To me, every hour of the day
and night is an unspeakably
perfect miracle.

WALT WHITMAN

Is it so small a thing to have
enjoyed the sun, to have lived
light in the spring, to have loved,
to have thought, to have done?

MATTHEW ARNOLD

Time, indeed, is a sacred little gift, and each day is a little life.

SIR JOHN LUBBOCK

Whether sixty or sixteen,
there is in every human being's
heart the lure of wonder, the unfailing
childlike appetite of what's next,
and the joy of the game of living.

SAMUEL ULLMAN

On your birthday—and all year round—I pray that your life will be chock-full of special moments. Take time to enjoy life. Don't be so busy you forget to notice a sunset or a child's smile.
And be good to yourself.

God has amazing things
in store for you.

ELLYN SANNA

The art of being happy lies in the power of extracting happiness from common things.

HENRY WARD BEECHER

To be glad of life because it
gives you the chance to love and to
work and to play and to look up at
the stars. . .to think. . .often of
your friends, and every day of
Christ. . .these are little guideposts
on the footpath of peace.

HENRY VAN DYKE

When grace is joined with wrinkles,
it is adorable. There is an unspeakable
dawn in happy old age.

VICTOR HUGO

Trust steadily in God,
hope unswervingly, love extravagantly.
And the best of the three is love.

1 CORINTHIANS 13:13 MSG

Have a wonderful birthday!
I'm thinking of you today.

"The LORD bless you and keep you;
the LORD make his face shine
upon you and be gracious to you;
the LORD turn his face toward
you and give you peace."

NUMBERS 6:24–26 NIV